OBSIDIAN SUN

OBSIDIAN SUN

A Poetry Compilation of Fiery Blackness
Written By Tyler Jones

For permission requests, contact Tyler Jones at MrJonesForeverMore@gmail.com.
Silver Bangles Productions books may be purchased for educational, business, or sales promotional use at www.silverbanglesproductions. com. For more information, please email info@silverbanglesproductions.com

Book Cover by Alex Joseph
Printed in Atlanta, GA, U.S.A.
First Printing, December 2025
Library of Congress Cataloguing-in-Publication Data is available on file
ISBN: 979-8-9888463-7-6

TABLE OF CONTENTS

OBSIDIAN SUN

~The tale of Blackness through fire, burns, stars, and the sun itself~

Remember to look it straight in the eyes and never lose your sight.

Because when you're looking/staring at Black excellence, you just might.

ENDORSEMENTS

Tyler is what the world needs more of. Passionate, creative, and caring. He stitches his words seamlessly together in hopes of wrapping you up in a cocoon of acknowledgment, understanding, and connection. He is a fantastic writer who sees the world, holds up a mirror, and says, *"Do you see you and your beauty?"* Through hardships and good times, his words show us that we are not alone and that we can win together.

- Cyan Villanueva, author of *The Lover's Fortune Vol. 1*

Obsidian Sun is a deeply moving debut that feels ancestral, like stories lovingly passed down through generations, recited with reverence and care. Each poem echoes with the strength of memory and the brilliance of legacy, reminding us that even through grief and generational trauma, we will continue to shine. This collection is both familiar and uplifting, offering encouragement, affirmation, and a glowing testament to the resilience we inherit and pass on. It is, without question, a love letter to Blackness, one that burns long after the final page.

- Micah Grace, author of *Echoes of Emptiness*

Powerful and poignant, Tyler Jones' *Obsidian Sun* celebrates his Blackness while acknowledging the painful past and history of Black people. Jones' rich imagery beautifully blends pain and power, providing poetry that is intricately layered, incredibly meaningful, and utterly striking. In *Obsidian Sun*, Jones shows how he has learned to transform his embers into flames, honoring the magic in being a fire that can't be put out.

- Alexis M. Romo, author of *What Remains of My Heart*

DEDICATION

I dedicate this book to my parents. Even through their burns, they continued to foster my star until I got to shine on my own. I became my sun. I can only hope that, in others, I spark the fires they did for me.

To my mom, your son did it. You put down your pen because you bore the burden of carrying the torch as the eldest daughter, wife, and mother to me and my brother. I picked up the pen and began to write where you thought parts of the story ended.

To my dad, you were a star of guidance for my life. Sometimes, it's too bright for me to see your own dark days. I can only pray I continue to make you proud.

I love you both. Thank you.

-Tyler

INTRODUCTION

Black People are the people of the Sun. Burning
bright as fire in the sky. Stars that won't ever go out.
Even when they die. Love is in the fire. Scorching,
blessed earth. Suns are created in every wake. Fami-
lies are created in the cluster of stars that create gal-
axies. This is a dedication to the fire they make. The
burns from their fate. The stars they create. And
the suns that take their place. This is *Obsidian Sun*.

GENESIS

The Fire

I was always told

*Fire is too dangerous. Too untamed and out of control, it can destroy anything in its wake. That it should be avoided at all costs. Used when needed, but afterward, put out and not to gain life. But I disagree. I never saw fire as something that must be controlled or used. It should be something we work together on. Because fire... births life. It creates.
It burns through souls and makes the mold that's shaping generations. It's diverse in color and gives warmth to a home. It's so amazing that some call it magic.*

History of Fire

The darkness doesn't know
What we went through to
Catch that first glimpse of
A flickering, fleeting spark.
It took countless days, nights,
Lives to even peek at, not what it is,
But what it could be.

A potential, so to speak.
But they cut our tongues to
Prevent whispers from catching
Wildfire to the ears of the masses.
No glass half full could douse the
Dreams we strived to see but
Red lines were drawn to
Ultimately, leave our homes empty.

Time and time and time again
Fire couldn't spark, but hope was
Never lost on that glimpse we saw.
Then, finally, after so long
Prometheus came and fire was born.

Prometheus

We were titans of fire.
Creators, innovators who brought
Fourth flames of formulation for
Culture and established a
Country from concoctions crafted from
Charisma and hopeful desperation.

Hoping for reparations, we
Struck hard and fast.
Prophesying that our hard work would
Advance us past the problems of
Colorful melanin, we were
Helpless as they used our very own
Sparks to set us ablaze and
Chain us to rocks in infinite torment.

Eaten alive each day, we pray
We become the heroes that
Save ourselves from this pain.

First Fire

What does it mean to be first?
Going by the definition, it's
Defined by being before all.
Respecting the date, time, and
Order of said proceedings.

For fire, cavemen spent
Ages in awe of the hot spire.
Not utilizing a fraction of the fire,
They squandered the very
Potential that burned bright.
Eons crossed stars until new
Creators created cases to
Contain the creation carefully.

They're the ones that are
Remembered and raised
Respectfully, regardless of the
Proceedings presented previously.

Fire came and went, but the
Innovators invented intelligently
To create new forms of fire.
So why don't we start taking
Credit for the fires we light?

Firestarter

A flame can't be doused
Once it's been set.
No water, air, or earth
Can take it out at its best. It may start small
But over time, many witnesses.

Fiery greatness as it
Flares and shoots off like
Fireworks are doing the lord's work.
Ferociously bright, a
Sight for the first fire's eyes to
See the flames
Prometheus was set after generations of burning
Now all at once and
Forever above the rest.

Without Fire

In the absence of fire,
There is nothing.
The very Society crafted has fallen
Flat without the flames.
Water may signify the turning
Tides of change, but
Without fire, there is no spark that
Moves hearts to get us this far.

Stars, the pretty sights in the
Mysterious skies we hold high,
They are ultimately the fiery balls of light
That helps us reside in a temporary sanctuary
In this life.

As I was young, I was told
Black people come from the sun.
So I see fire when I look at us.
Because without black fire,
The country of red and white becomes a
Sad, blue, monotonous dump.

Warm Fires

Family.
A warmth that's never forgotten
But often missed when
Winters hit.
Battling through storms,
It's good to know that warm
Blooded cousins, give your
Heart something when life can feel
Soul-crushing.

All you need is a little love.
Mothers and brothers.
Sisters and fathers.
I may be far, but
My fires aren't.
Not at all.

When my fires live in my heart.
That's always home.

This Little Light

Darkness can be blinding.
Hiding what is meant to be
Seems to further bring the
Soul to height previously
Never reached.

Discouraging daggers from words draw
Blood, but I've never tired or
Discouraged when I spark
Small fires from memories.
Light is shining for me to see.

Sparks Fly

Synchronized fires
Burn brighter when they
Form a union, but who is to
Say that fire doesn't burn Hard and fast before it's
Blown out something crass.
There's a risk of merging
Their lights, but the risk is
Worth it.
So let's burn tonight.

Charming Charcoal

Pressure makes diamonds, but we
Shine in the darkest of nights and
Brightest of days.
Forever beautiful.
Gleaming, that's what it takes a
View full and encapsulates
Generations upon generations of
Culture and creation culminate in
Creatures of curation.
Adding to everything they touch,
Charcoal folks come in many different forms,
Shades and despite the shade,
They always find a chance to shine.
Creating fires, we burn bright in
Flames until there's rain to
Stop our rainbow reign.

Fire We Make

There's passion in these matches.
They strike a hot chord
With every match scorched.
Burning quickly and fast,
We try to make each moment last.
But these are matches after all,
They are not meant to be
More than that.
In these lights,
We make our nights full of
What we might be if we could
Make these matches into lamps.
Only then would we know
What it's like to turn our fires
Into something more than a
Night for our hearts to set camp.

Right of Fire

Under this sun,
No fire is equal.
It's the opposite of
What was said but the
Truth of what is practiced.
Preaching isn't even
Necessary when I have
Examples that continue to
Lose their breath.

There aren't any
Sparks left.

But even as the small
Candles are blown out
I see fires that refuse to
Be set aside and doused.
They're fighting for their right.

To burn. To breathe. To a life.
And that, is their right.

Matches

The warmth of other suns
Could never match your soul.
Setting fire to those around you
I always want to surround you,
That is the match to start mine.
I thought my moon
Desperately needed your radiant
Light for my heart to shine.

The warmth created when it
Touched yours is unmatched.
As time went by, I kept using yours
Only to see yours run out. Feeding off
What you freely gave was unhealthy
For me and you.
I only knew how to
Take my stunted growth,
Which stunted your further development.
Your light.
For that, I can match what
You gave me.

I promise not only to give
Back, but better, refuel yours and
Find the match I thought I never had.
Instead, I douse the match to turn on

The lamp to illuminate my eyes
To see the path I should've
Been on all along.
Synthesized Fire

Faux flames face fate, fearing
Destruction is soon to be their
Consequences of the animosity
Fanned by their fires and the
Futures are hindered by their envy.

The sun never liked fools who
Flew too close without paying
Pretty pennies for sunny cities.

The Price of Fire

Inflation is steadily rising
As the creative market
Harps on onyx tinged
Artists to light their past on
Fire until the trauma crisps
Skin until they whittle away.
Flake by flake, the flames
Erode the bits of my soul
I tried to hide and hold close.
But in times that find
Words fueled by fossils,
12 Years a slave is more
Appealing than feelings of Black happiness that
would
Surely bring a smile to the face.
Our frowns stay upright,
Before they go upside down
As I push this bleak, depressing
Charcoal looks like a sad clown.
In the end, pain for profit
Continues to burn

The Sun's Fire

God greets gold
in all her glory.
Seeing a sight that gets the
heart soaring above the skies.
As every sight of her
makes my ambitions take flight to
shine as bright as the giver of heat.
She brings me close to home—to warmth
I thought was lost.
Only the night controls her glow,
yet her influence grows in her absence
to freeze progress in her wake.
I write for her sake.
Or I will break—knowing I'd be forsaken
if I awaken Apollo's mistress
through unapologetic distress.
Burning brighter than any star in the sky
I won't lose sight of her might.
The sun's muse has my heart
as she helps me make my days start
As long as she's in sight.

Valley of Flames

Starving for water, I get hotter with each
Step I take as my body is set ablaze on the
Road you presented as I go inside your
Valley of pent-up aggression. Blood stained
Battles left scars around your walls, but
Outside your cool exterior lies an inside of
Passionate pain that flows behind love you hide.
I go deeper with each taste you provide.

Finding treasures that are bittersweet, I
See the core of your heart leak through your
Pores, as I get sweet sweat to fill the glass, I
Drink from before I enter the furnace. You are
Burning the environment to ash so it can
Revive itself and fly above the previous
Past life they once had. A proponent of
Change that does her best to shine her light
When she doesn't want to shine all the time.

Finally accepting all the fire she hides, we are
One and I realize she's been open the whole time.
I hold her tight, and she wraps around us
Forever to hold the other secure in the flames
Between her thighs. Burning until the crisp
Burns black and lying in the ground to rest for
Death isn't the last time we're alive, so we
Rise from our ashes to take forever flight.

JUDGES

Our Burns

Feel the burn.

I mean, no pain, no gain, right? But what if that pain is too much to bear and the rules I once saw as fair have left me smoldering from my skin to my core? It's horrific. Seeing what was once considered beautiful is now blistering in bubbles that are about to burst from burns that burn blue from the boiling heat. I beseech whoever made this world blue for Black people. Beaten until the burns blossom into many different forms, I'm torn. After so long, we might have learned to love the burn.

Scar vs. Burn

Marks of pain
Are not made the same
Nor do they heal that way.

Stitch me back together
From all the times you cut me off
Or cut me down.
The skin forms back in a line
With lines sewn into a stitched frown.
A monster I'm living with
From your Frankenstein smile.

Sear me until the burn is home,
Knowing whatever used to be there
Is burnt down and gone.
Skin that has taken its place
Makes me look at myself in shame
Unable to trace what I saw before,
A piece of me has been displaced.

Healed in unique ways, but
Forever not the same
To never forget the pain.

Where There's Smoke

The smell is apparent.
It's hard to miss.
Intoxicatingly pungent to the
Point that it burns when it
Fills your lungs with sooty mist.
Spreading and engulfing
All that's in its path.
It's not red wrath, but it's
Labeled as a Black Plague the
Way it slays in its wake.
I call it fate.
Using oxygen for fuel,
Building upon missing fossils
Some call it cruel.
But it's culture.
The smoke comes from fire
And we all smell it
But who lit the match?
We'll let the fire tell it.

The House Is Burning

Peek inside the windows to witness the
Fahrenheit rise for little fires everywhere
Can no longer hide as each book of
Memories burn with no remorse for my mind.

Previously, pouring water on oil burns
Sear and scar until I can only say,
"This is fine," for I can't lie, but I've grown
Accustomed to the life of burnt hides. No
Tears can come if they evaporate before a
Sigh of relief is cried. I can't hide.

Smoke signals mimic the screens I've
Put around my life, but they are now
Visible for every eye, but I refuse to cower
Behind the flames, as I embrace it all.

A benign blaze of bright light as the pure white
Fears burn black to completion. The
"I'm Fine" isn't the self-believed lie, and I know
When my house burns, it's no longer a fright.
My little world isn't the only one set on fire,
We burn in unison, refusing fight or flight.

Face the Sun

Best to go about face when it's hard to
Face what has been done after
Years of trauma boil the blood.
Piping over, the skin blisters in wrenching,
Searing pain that even
Shadows can't darken.
Feeling the heat, but fearing the burn
They are afraid to face the scorn.
The seething hatred.
Possibly going blind from the light,
Eyes avoid what's been done to just
Tan and refuse to do what's right.
Building brick houses to
Hide away from all that's been done,
Pale-faced sinners are afraid to face the sun.

Crash & Burn

Flames present and housed in my lungs
Suffocate me slowly in lonely smoke
But at least I feel something
Anything after the nerves were ice burned.
Not being able to crack and bleed
Took more life out of me.
A house isn't a home if
Not a soul is alive to call it that
Including my own.
This fire is alive and gives me scorching,
Searing warmth to the bone.
In this death,
I'm finally not alone.
Getting high off this carcinogen smoke
As this soul gets to crash and burn.

27 Million Degrees

You can't touch us.
We run too hot.
If you're not careful
You will get burned.
There's no doubt about that.
But from afar,
You must still be careful.
Eyes can't handle the
Star in front of them.
Might go blind trying to
Stop and stare at the
Star defying gravity in the air.
But in your hesitation
Don't shun the sun.
We're hot to the touch
But we give warmth
Worth a million suns.
27 million Fahrenheit
On the surface, but
Cold core from no love.

Suntan

Summer suns give my skin
Extra melanated love, but
When it's all said and done
Orange skin is more
Idolized than my beautiful,
Bold charcoal. I set fire to
Magazines in my home.

Sunburn

Liquid protection only
Lasts so long until the
Skin dries up from its
Sunny drought in the
Face of doubt left by
Burning situations of
Apparent racial ambiguity.

Burn Marks

Trauma truly doesn't leave. It
Sears its mark deep. Piercing
Through the skin and into your
Heart. Scar tissue that leaves long
Lasting issues, we try our best to
Cover and hide, but the pain sometimes
Makes us out of character in
Real-time. Aloe Vera bandages wrap the
Wound tight. In hopes that the
Skin won't be as sensitive as we
Continue to walk on our path of life.

Daughters of Suns

Protected but often publicly
Disrespected, a sisterhood of
Light that's thrown shade amongst
Black holes that suck away their
Bright auras into nothing
But there are supernovas
Burning bright from the planetary
System of stellar nebulas that
Propelled pillars of purposeful
Polished spheres that lead,
Organize and recognize their
Worth to push stars in the making.

Flickering Rage

One spark.
That's all it takes.
And it spreads.
First, like a slow
Build that burns
Each and every fiber.
Then it quickens to a
Numbing blitz that
Corners every nerve
Until flares of red
Fill black corneas to
Lay waste in fiery rage.
But before it starts,
Sirens are called to
Cease the flames
In any way they can
Before the sparks
Burn down the forest
And truly feel what
Being burnt black in
America is, insane.

Too Close to the Sun

Hopes and dreams exist
Because they're currently not a reality.
We aspire to aim higher
For all that we don't have.
Shining in the middle of the night
Guiding us to stars that ultimately
Won't last.
By the time we're close
Sunshine illuminates to hide
Those dreams we had once seen.
Burning our bodies
And melting our wings
To fall like Icarus
From burnt hopes and dreams.

Black Fire

What does it mean to
Burn black as hell?
Is it to incinerate until
Total evisceration leaves
Charcoal of a soul to
Fuel ivory fantasies from
Obsidian dreams, or is it
Eternal ebony embers
Embodying the essence of
Life that continues to
Shift culture and hide
Away from vultures vying to
Steal from its progenitors?
Or is it simply the last
Match in the box, trying to
Save its fire for life?
Guess I'll light myself to
See how I burn tonight.

Burning Away Bits of Self

Balance is hard to maintain
when the
Two halves lose control and
start to
Eat away at the very fabric that
held you
Together each day. Devouring
parts that
Kept you whole and away
from the
Hole you continuously dug
yourself in.
After each time you collected
losses and
Refused to recognize the
many wins
In each bite, tearing you apart until
they have
Gotten the last taste of what it was meant
to be.
You and the rest are in a
blazing, burning
State to ultimately stay safe
even if.
Whatever you thought was left
is saved.

Melted Mask

Serene suns stare back at me.
Seeing the paint drip from my
Face tearfully, it pities what I
Tried to hide behind white lies.
Building over time to create a
White face that blended in the
White sea of faces who hate me.

Hell's Children

They say hell is hot, but when the
Flames become home, how do I
Even know when something is
Wrong?

Odds are I'm already burnt to a
Crisp, and my soul is a wisp of
What I used to be. Its fire has
Grown dim in hopes it will learn
How to cope when there's no
Hope.

Despair is all that's there, but
Who says that I can't ascend
Beyond the smoke they blow to
Raise temperatures of the
Places that I've all known are
Home?

Breaking the glass ceiling to
Contain my own fire, I rise and
Reign atop the heavens as I was
Meant to be, and I can see hell
May be where I started, as an

Eternity of prejudice was
Never meant for people of the
Sun.
Burning Ferocious Fire

We burn hot and fast.
But
Sometimes too fast as we
Begin to lose life and grow dim.
We light up rooms.
But
Sometimes too bright as
People try to steal it.
We provide warmth.
But
Sometimes too much as
Friends take advantage.
We are extinguished.
Because we bring
So much to this world
But
We don't care.
Fire doesn't fear.
It only lives and goes.

For it doesn't waver to water.
It only grows.

Blinded by Fire

Seared eyes don't see much,
But the fire that caused the
Loss of sight and reason
Of a mind gone mad.
Rage can't last if
Cooled by healing waters,
But if the streams never come
It's an eternal summer sun
Burning all you had.
I'm hot.
I'm mad.

Firewater

Extinguished in the raging seas
See me gasping for air where
Oxygen breathes just enough
Life into my light, trying to stay
Afloat in hopes that boiling
Waters don't take me under.

Each gulp, my lungs break
Apart of my self-confidence
But I can see the shore in the
Middle of these dark nights. I
Bite down and burn bright
Until I can take what is mine.

Black Phoenix

Rising from the ashes is contrived
after seeing your brethren
continue to die.
Being told to rise above is hard when
captors don't let you get far
once they take your feathers and
cage you off from the others that helped you
burn bright like the sons and daughters
suns loved to hug and
fly across the seas they were forced to travel.
Saying we are a hassle complaining when
we didn't want to be on a land
that we still thrived in.
Now they want us hiding.
I say no.
We we will not find comfort in the cages
you hold
but we will instead grow and
break free from the mold.
Black phoenixes rise above
but not because you told us so.

Fiery Fate

There's a delicacy and fragility
In allowing oneself to be burned.
Owning the incinerating feeling
Fire breathes upon the skin.
If my people are called demons
Hell never felt so nice.
No ice needed to cool my sin.
I find pride in that
I was born with sin.
Burning was our fate;
A generation meant to be
Consumed by tumultuous fire.
Knowing with each challenge
The smoke gets a little higher.

Flames are Home

*There's something magical about how Black burns in
the fire.
Charcoal skin enhances each flame
As it sings gloriously in generational pain
And it's a shame rain doesn't
Live anywhere near where the fires are kept
But we all know how they were set.
Some even argue we burn
When we're at our best.*

*Black turns a melancholy blue
As the fires turn white hot under the
Dark of the Moon and its
Reflecting beautifully as we make
What is do and we do what we must
Because it's all we can do.
Peace in the fire of eternal summers
Hoping winter comes to cool the
Bodies burned after white wonder.*

*Fires won't be home forever
When change comes rolling like thunder.*

More Than the Flames

When you touch me, do you feel
More than the fire from my skin?

When you see me, can you look
Pass the environment I was raised in?

When you hear me, can you listen
To my intentions ingrained in my vernacular?

Burning hot from the things people
Say, and I want to react, but then you
Combat the reality I live in when
Media runs it like a grotesque play.
Fearmongers who walk to the
Other side of the street with a straight face smile,
Hiding their lips in an
Awkward diss to what I represent.

I'm more than the fire you're afraid of.
My melanin is beautiful. It is love.
Obsidian gold, you're blessed to
Witness, and see how we shape this
World into a sight beautiful to behold.

PSALMS
Shining Stars

When I looked up,

I was always happy to see the stars that came before me. Not really recognizing their impact until their fall, but still admiring every twinkle that made wrinkles in the sky. Sometimes clouds would hide their light, but I know the history behind every one that shone in the night. How each one fought until the day they came crashing down in flight. I'm proud to be one of them, and hopefully someday, I'll add to the pantheon of gorgeous celestial clusters. Among my sisters and brothers, I'll live forever until the dead light is remembered throughout stories in time.

Royal Stars

Luminous, rich heavenly bodies
Embodying what it means to be
Kings, queens, royalty in seas
Drenched in divine drips of
Black, brown, caramel christened
Skin that blends with blue, but
Glistens in golden rays on display.

Twilight's Funeral

Waiting in the water of mourning,
The sun has gone down on
Another star whose light could
No longer fight the encroaching dark.
We bury the heart at the
Impending dusk and pray the
Stars call you home as you
Forever roam the skies in new life.
Tears, I fear, approach my eyes
As Here, My Dear lullabies
My cries fade into the background.
I know I'll see you around,
But only after my sun goes down.

Dead Stars

They say I'm shooting
But I'm really falling.
They pray for my demise
To manifest their wishes.
One by one, I see
My brothers and sisters
Dropping like flies, but
We shine brighter.
Each of us in white
With our families in black
Mourning our crash.
I'm just glad with death,
We made an impact.

Shattered Star

Glass shards of fire scorch
Marks into history from not being
Whole after generations.
Suffering from a lack of
Formation, our passion
Fragments into contrasting forms of
Colors of painted glass that
Stains the possibility of reparations.
But after so much time apart,
Ideas of what they need are
Distinctively different and
Have to find their piece of the
Pie if their fire is to burn bright.
But in this sky, I'm not
Sure if they will find the
Fuel to fly to do us right.

Constellation of the Fallen

Year by year,
Each iota of light grows brighter
After each blink of focus.
There's been an understanding of self
And ancient ancestry that coincides
Years before my time.
After another one of us has been taken,
They are given back to me
In a form that I can see
But can't touch.
Far from my hand
Yet I feel their love.
Coming together to form a matriarch
Lying in the night sky.
Watching and waiting for my
Eventual greatness they birthed.
Creating a coalition of seeds that
Reached new heights.
The fallen stars are my keepers
As I keep them in sight.
Even when it's dark,
I continue to see their light.

Celestial Family

It's awe-inspiring to be
Immortalized in the
Heavens we know as the sky.
A far cry from how we were
Known when we were alive.
Each twinkle creates a
Wrinkle in memories for our
Legacy to be carried. Hopefully,
Reminding our descendants to be
Wary of those intentions that are to
Ultimately leaves you buried
Amongst the stars you admire.
Far away balls of fire that will
Remain forever remembered as long as
We sing of their bright, blue murders.
Cursed as shiny, inspiring martyrs.

Eclipse

Stars don't always shine.
Sometimes they hide.
Fearing the light they bring,
Days come when they don't
Want to be seen. Letting
Fools block their view but
Only a few seconds can
Create this new moon as
Building light brews their
Blessings for a slew of
Greatness to peer through
Eyes that realize a sight
Beholden a star to debut.

Nap of a Star

Can you see me
Hiding in the dark?
Light far from the
Eyes who try to find
The hidden me.
Brighter beings catch the
Attention of those
Looking through the long
Lens searching for
More than meets their
Eyes. Deliverance among
Skies of light they cry
When the light falls and
Dies at their feet. But they
Wished for it from the
Beginning for its end.

So I hide

Afraid to see what
Embracing my light
Will find among the sky.
Knowledgeable me stays
Sleep even when I'm
Forever woke to the
Darkness around me.
But in the black painted
Life, there's blues to be
Pronounced and reds
Painted amongst our
Backdrops of life.
So instead of hitting
Snooze, the nap is
Over and the light
I hid inside has time
To be just as beautiful
In the vast overhead sea.
Moons and suns can't
Hold me back from
Having you see the
Bright I hid from me.
Flipping the switch was
Always the solution to
Light the star you were
Always meant to see.

Wish Upon a Star

It's hard to believe all their
Hopes and dreams rest on me.
First to college, first to graduate
First to make it past the area of
Desolate and depressing poverty.
Shoulders feel heavy and legs
Sink sadly in sands from the
Time passed from sunken
Possibilities and the reality isn't that I'm
First to be able but the first
Star given the fuel to even have a
Chance to burn and I'm blessed.
I just hope I don't fall from a
Form of shooting from
Wishing on my downfall. Don't
Wish upon this star.

Star's Wishes

I've always dreamed of
Being one of the stars.
Until I was one.
Always being watched
With nowhere to hide, I
Wait for the sun to shine
So I don't seem as bright.

Under the spotlight
I try to hide my other
Side so others can't find
Me. Scrutiny, judgement, hate
Makes me isolate
Myself among other stars
So I don't go too far
From my place I hold
Dear. Close to my heart.

For if I'm going to shine
I need my space in the
Dark. Black shines brightest
In my dark. My space. My
Place. Where I can be
Me. And not expect more than
What they see.

A person who finds comfort
In what I've come to be.
A star who finds comfort
In knowing we are all stars.
Not letting anyone dictate
What we can be. And I'm
Loving what we're becoming.

So I'm embracing my shine
And I know you're seeing me.

Love of a Star

Thank you for existing.
I mean that truly.
With every ounce of my
Heart that's bound to stop.
It beats passionately for your
Fire in the sky.
I don't know what you've done,
But it doesn't matter.
You exist, and you bring
Joy by just being there.
Alive. Thriving. Surviving.
Not for anyone else.
Just for you.
And for that,
I thank you.

Star Power

Don't ever forget the
Sky you were raised in.
It wasn't just a place to
Play in before you
Blew up after all your wins.
You have grown and shown
Promises create galaxies,
Molding stars of your own.
But a star without purpose
Can grow into a black hole.
With that said, don't turn into a
White dwarf burning on its
Last set of matches.
Remember what made you,
And give back to the masses.

Every Nigga Is A Star

As we proceed to
Give you what you need,
Black stars rise and
Feed the culture daily.
Half past crazy, our
Desire to raise empires have
Gained much profit for the
Star bangled vultures that
Holster the dreams of
Exploited ebony artists for ages.
Our rage, our love, our trauma,
Lead to multi-million commas
Pocketed rarely by those who
 Scream the loudest.
Each star that walked to fame
Have roots in a craft that was
Originally ordained in disdain
"For colored only."
But without the colored contribution,
This nation would be pretty boring.
Twinkling and burning
Right in front of us,
Black stars shine until they are
Turned into angel dust.

Star With a Story

When my child looks to the
Sky, I hope they look up and
See me. The parent I strove to be
Was one that they could
Cry to when the moon wasn't
Looking and the dark, bright
Light of my eyes kept the tears
Away at night. I pray that
When they're lost, I'm the
Guiding star to bring them
Out of the pitch blackness to
Show them their black is the
Right way to fight off forces of
White that might try to purge
Paths laid before them. That
Kid of mine knows the Star they
Strive to be won't be me but
Use my star to make the star
Their kids will strive to be. So
Stories won't die when my light
Passes, and there will always be
Stars with stories with various
Tales for all my kids' kids to read.

REVELATIONS
We Are Suns

The world runs from the rays of the people of the Sun, but just when you think we're done. *The ice in my heart has melted, and I'm flooding over with emotion. The notion that light would always be eclipsed has broken. We're divine sunshine in the corner of every room. Never look at the rainy days and say we're through. Without the rain, there's no rainbow, and our rays give us hope. Beautiful. Intelligent. Amazing. That's how Black people do.*

Sunrise

Morning after morning
I must rise.
There's no option
Otherwise if I decide to
Not. There is no try
Only do. Even when
Days turn to nights
There's no use
Fighting what I'm
Meant to when I
Rise. My sunshine
Flies through the
Skies to touch every
Inch of earth and
Heaven greets me
As I rise. Another
Day, another dollar
Comes with time and I
Realize even if I fall
I will always rise.
Please lift me high
Never forget me
When I rise and a
New sun takes my
Shine to rise again.

Violet in the Sun

Purple Hearts of loyalty to my
Melanin royalty that holds me
Joyously in high regard.

I have come far to plant
Flowers that have blossomed
Thanks to the blood poured to
Nourish my growth in hopes
I become better than them.

The soil grows richer from
Rotating the crops and the
Suns that came before gave
Life so that I might shine
No matter the downpour.

Petals drip gleefully knowing my
Roots run deep in history.

Under the Sun

Once upon a dawn,
From the ground grew a
Son. Watered and cared,
It knew no other one.

Ideal time spent under
Clear sky's until
Cloudy days let me know
What it truly meant to
Pay. Time spent where
I'm from, I just needed
One sun. But when it's
Clouded, my thoughts are
Shrouded and the growth
Wanted wasn't what I
Flaunted. A shadow cast
Under the one that gave me
Hope, all the progression
Went down the slope.
Nope. It's not ideal,
But burnt feelings left
The Exterior crispy.

Unsatisfied under
Rays of eyes, disappointed
I cried hoping to show the

Other side. Soft and
Tender moments filled
Interiors to be exposed
After being eaten away.

So I hope and pray this
Son is shown another day.

First Sun

Two stars came alive when I
Opened my eyes. A sight for sore eyes
Who Started this marriage happy but
Dried lies would later bring sighs
When their love didn't burn as bright.

Being their first combined sun, I
Needed to burn bright to always
Show their wasn't a one off and was
Greater than the original sum but their
Second was the one destined to come.

Planning is easy when you decide but
Surprises are the ones that truly rise.
Being the oldest I was expected to be
Mild while being extraordinary and
Lead my whole life in single file.

How disappointing was it to find the
First was nothing but boringly ordinary.
Second times the charm as the second
Found the light to burn hearts with
Passion as my partners lost compassion.

Not in me for they always loved the first,
But the second had attention that wasn't

Quite like mine. Growing dimmer, I
Hid away in the cold until I found comfort
Isolating away from the star's hold.

Years went by and then I felt ruined once I
Saw the sun that came up first was a
Moon soon to be gone and pruned, but
Bounced back he found he could shine
Even in the dark. His heart wasn't lost.

Sun and moon, working side by side.
Each having strengths and weaknesses
Others took in stride. Not always getting
Along but realizing together they're strong,
Two suns shone bright in their song.

First Rays of Light

Cries resound throughout the
Room as I get to hold you in
Arms shaking hysterically
But I hold you steady and
Firm to show you daddy
Won't let you fall
No matter how much this
World shakes and turns.
Opening your eyes I get a
Glimpse of yours that
Burn brightly from the
Stars your mother and I
Birthed for a life we yearned.
Brown and black in all your
Glory, the world may not be
Ready for you and if they
Try to take you from us, they
Will be sorry.
Beautifully born a combination of
Colors that shine so bright, I'm
Thankful and proud of this
Little light and hope and pray
You'll be safe and burn
Proudly in the day and night.

Let the Sun Shine

Is it so hard to be happy
For someone else's success?
Letting ones magic or joy
Be sullied by unnecessary noise
Is a crime when it's hurting the
Futures of young girls and boys.
They should be looking up to the
Stars stretched by the suns
That came before and say
"I want more,"
Before clouds come and block
Light from reaching their core.
I want them to pop.
I want them to blow.
Show everything they can be
Before I have to go.
Let the children be kids
And not some little adult.
Let them shine as
Long as they can
As we help them grow.

To My Future Sun

Don't forget where you come from
As you continue to shine on. There will be
Those who try to damper what
You bring to the room but there is
Nothing and I mean
Nothing
That can stop you from being you,
Unless it's you.
Sometimes we're our own worst
Enemy, and we burn too bright to
See what our reflection is trying to show who or
What you're meant to be.
Don't get lost in your own
Heat to burnout from the inside and be
Stuck outside of your destiny.
A star.
In your own right and sometimes you
Will spit flames to be seen
But don't let the eyes that blinded by your
Blinding light make you forget where
You come from.
You come from me. You come from us.
So be the best you can be.
A sun from the people of suns.
Being all you can be.

Son of Suns

Falling off our predecessors
Dew of light, we burned
Small but grew from purple
Nebulas into blue giants
Shining beautifully at night.

Learning from the dwarfed
History of those who came
Before, our red rage left our
Fires white hot until our souls
Stewed into supernovas.

Scorching everything in our
Path, we eventually had to
Stop and see the destruction
Stars had made. I'm sad to
Say we burned into black holes.

No neutron to make us whole.

Like Father, Like Sun

I want to be a better sun
Than the son who raised me.
Lighter in the moments you
Wanted me to be brighter.
Giving warmth when you
Believed I should be hotter.
Being a star to guide
But you said I need to lead.
All these lessons and more
But don't get it twisted.
While I find myself
Putting out the fires you created,
Embers in my ashes crafted
A new sense of self esteem.
I love how you pushed me
To turn my small candle
Into a bombastic bonfire.
Grabbing parts that
Increased my fire,
Discarding coals that
Suppressed and seared my soul.
I'm my father's son who
Became a sun before his eyes.
Now I'll be a sun to the
Stars who will light up my sky.

Mother of Suns

My forever guiding light in a
Life that was given to us by you.
Forever grateful, We're
Faithful and devoted to the
Queen of suns that found it
Hard to shine in the darkest of days
And the brightest of nights.
Never allowing us to lose a fight,
You helped us choose life
When we didn't want to.
Picking us up from the door of
Death and despair, you
Bared your heart not only for us
But for the world to stop and stare.
Not blinding, but comforting in her warmth.
A mother of suns that
Adorn their mother forever more.

Let the Sun Talk

Often times,
The sun wants to shine but
Clouds are cast.
Never allowing a drop of
Light to brighten their days,
Something always gets in the way.
Reprimanding their rights,
The sun won't go
Down without a fight.
Even if in battle,
They end up losing their life.
But what they don't know,
Even when a sun falls
Suns rise again to twinkle
In the midst of nightfall.
Suns talk and gleam,
Refusing to back down to
Always be seen.

Last Light

It was truly a flash before my eyes.
The flickering loss of life.
I feel my fire is losing its light
After each blink of my iris but
Before I go, I want to
Reflect on my life's kindness.
Not always nice, my fire
Waned under the night. Sometimes
Scared of faces who
Envied my light but I decided to
Never dim my brightness.
No matter the fight.
I passed the torch over time to
Create a village that lit up
Roads that I only attempted to
Walk down and I'm proud they do.
Candles grew to flames as
We sang and used the oxygen to
Increase our flames to make a
Family that will forever reign.
My flame is now a flicker
But I'm surrounded by many suns.
As I close my eyes,
My light doesn't go out
But joins the eternal one.

Solar Power

There's power in togetherness.
Hence why the powers that be try to
Constantly write decrees to stop the
Powers of we. See there's power in a
Destined star and power in a singular
Sun but the fire in collective
Light finds one fist in the sky.
Raised high. Fighting for life, love, and
Whatever our light can touch. We will
Forever bring blessings upon us.

The Sun is Human Too

Just because we shine bright
Don't forget shade can be
Thrown our way each and
Every day the sun says "hey."

People think we're magic
But I'll tell you what, magic
Still lives under the microscope
Hoping our magic is smoke.

Magnifying glasses that
Make us put fire to asses
And they were the crass ones
When they get guns to blast us.

Suns are suns and what we
Do is amazing but just because
Suns shine bright, don't belittle
Suns before we go out blazing.

Sun Sessions

Different terms of burns
Black on my skin as each
Turn of the sun during
Summer sees this star
Scorch my brown earth.

Each singe gives birth to
Lines of ash I lotion to
Soften my iron exterior
For my silky interior that
Some deem inferior.

Superiority raised by
False moon idols that
Shine white at night won't
Dampen my obsidian
Dreams of a son black.

Sunkissed

Delicate pecks that sit
Delicately on my skin
Every morning as the
Morning star recites
Love songs on every
Pore, it's blissfully sore.

SunDrunk

Sugary, serene sun sweetly
Sweeps me off my feet when
She smiles so brightly at me.
Secretly only shining melanin
Seas on each pore, It will never
Sear my skin and it will only
See me when during sessions of
Sensational sentiments of love.
Seeking to protect our peace,
Sun rays get me drunk so I'm
Sipping satisfying skin sex.

Sol Circle

Illumination. Bright eyes light up my
Night as I stare into your golden rays of
Sunshine. You became my favorite
Color from long looks of love that radiated
Rainbows after the rain and you came to
Glow as the moon looked from above so
Below our past transgressions, we
Grew full circle into love that moved
Beyond pitiful notions of lust and lost
Sight of seasonal sessions of what we
Thought love costs. So we spend our time
Lying in our truths and waiting in glorious
Suns that we use to heat up nights that
Leave us in bed and experience what the
Touch of years of understanding can bring.

Obsidian Sunshine

There's a light inside my mind
Shining darkness to a black
Illumination everywhere in sight.
It's beautiful in its honesty,
Simple in its complexity, and
Warm in its completion. No
Season has its ownership to
Freely appear as it sees fit.
Hearts know enlightenment from
Experiencing its bloom, knowing
No matter the day, time, or place
Blackness will come soon and
All will love black sun as the moon.

Sundown

I'm tired. I'm starting to
Fade as the day wanes.
Bright lights change from
Godlike gold to opulent
Orange to resting red to
Peaceful purple to bashful
Blue once these hues have
Mutated to something new
When moons shade the day.
Resting my eyes, hoping to
Wake up to my lights play.

ACKNOWLEDGMENTS

Throughout the journey of writing this book, I felt lost. Truly, deeply lost on what I wanted to write. I first came up with the concept in the midst of 2020. Originally, my first book was going to be on something light and fun, but as I witnessed the hellscape that was 2020, I couldn't *not* talk about my people. Writing has been everything to me my whole life. When I didn't know what to do, writing was there for me. When I couldn't stand up for myself, writing picked me back up and helped me throw the first punch to self-doubt, racism, depression, and prevented death from taking me from my own two hands. God, family, and friends helped me foster my pen to where it is today. Lord willing, it will take me farther.

ABOUT THE AUTHOR

Tyler Auston Jones is a Black poet/writer based in Atlanta, Georgia. He was born in Dallas, Texas, in the fall of 1995. Always having the words but never the voice to speak them, writing became the avenue through which he expressed himself. To continue his discovery of self, past his words, Tyler moved to Greenville, North Carolina, to live with his father. There, he graduated from high school at J.H. Rose High School and got his Bachelor's in English with a creative writing minor from Western Carolina University. He moved to Atlanta the same year of his graduation to start his career in writing.

After working in online music journalism, he transitioned to education in 2021. Always a staunch supporter of Blackness and its history in America, Tyler came up with the concept for *Obsidian Sun* back in 2022. He's been published in Contemporary Verse 2, Fahmidan Journal, and Hyacinth Review, among others, for his poetry.

Connect with the Author Online
Instagram: @taj.the.poet
Twitter/X: @tajthepoet95
Substack: Musings of My Mind
Website: penmeetslife.com